Hi friends. At school we have been learning about idioms. I didn't know what an idiom was before.
When I heard someone say a silly phrase, it didn't make any sense! I thought that they had jumbled up their words!

Hmm..

Idioms are phrases and silly sayings that we sometimes use. They do not always make sense, so they can sound very confusing! They are something that we can learn! Let's learn some together and have some fun! Are you ready? Some of these are very funny!

'It's raining cats and dogs' means,
that it is raining heavily!

'Get your skates on' means let's hurry up and get moving.

'Pull your socks up' means come on.. make an effort!

The 'bees knees' means something or someone is excellent.

You are the bees knees!

Watch your step!

When someone says 'watch your step' they are asking you to be careful not to trip or walk into anything.

'Under the weather' means someone doesn't feel very well.

'To have a frog in the throat' means that someone needs to cough or clear their throat. Their voice may sound a bit croaky.

'From the bottom of your heart' means that you mean something sincerely. You really mean something with so much love.

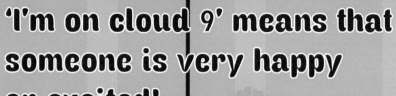

'I'm on cloud 9' means that someone is very happy or excited!

'Bob's your uncle' is a silly phrase to explain when something is easy or a task can be achieved! I bet you were thinking, 'who's Bob?'

The phrase 'pigs might fly' is said to explain that certain things will never happen!

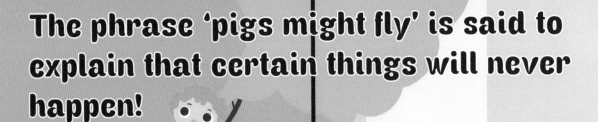

I can jump over that tree!

Oh yeah, pigs might fly!

When we say 'piece of cake'
it means that something is easy
to do or achieve.
Although, some cake would be nice!

To 'sit on the fence' really means that the person is not sure which choice to choose.
They are undecided.

Hmm
I'm on the fence with this.

What is she talking about sitting on a fence for?

'To let the cat out of the bag' means, to tell everyone a secret or an idea.

If someone says they have 'brain freeze' they have eaten very cold ice cream or had a very cold drink. Then they might have a funny feeling in their head afterwards!

When someone says, 'spill the beans' they would like you to tell them the secret!

Ooh spill the beans then!

'A chip off the old block' means, that the person is very similar to their mother or father.

If someone says they are 'as cool as a cucumber' it means they are feeling relaxed and calm.

If something costs an 'arm and a leg' they mean that it will cost them a lot of money.

'Barking up the wrong tree' means, that we have misunderstood something or have got something completely wrong.

We say we have 'butterflies in our tummy' if we are feeling nervous, worried or excited.

There are so many funny idioms to learn.
I am still learning them too!
I know they are very confusing,
but it is fun to learn them!
Which one was your favourite idiom?
It's been really fun sharing new things
with you! I mean that from the bottom
of my heart!

Printed in Great Britain
by Amazon

79425854R00018